LEGENDS OF

THE OHIO VALLEY;

or

THRILLING INCIDENTS

OF

INDIAN WARFARE.

TRUTH STRANGER THAN FICTION.

BY JAMES H. McMECHEN.

WHEELING:

WEST VIRGINIA PRINTING COMPANY, PRINTERS.

1887

Table of Contents

PREFACE.

The author deems it proper to say, that the term "Legend," used in the title of this book, is not to be taken in the sense of that which is fictitious or doubtful, but of that which is strictly historical and true; and, although the events narrated are, in point of fact, believed to be strictly true, yet there are many incidents connected with them of such marvelous character as to touch not only the romantic but the sublime of personal daring and moral heroism. Hence he has preferred the title of "Legends."

The object of this book is to present to the public a faithful record of some of the most thrilling events connected with the border wars carried on for several years between the whites and the Indians in the Valley of the Upper Ohio.

In carrying out this purpose, he has endeavored as much as possible, to derive his information from original sources, and from the best authors. Without further reference it may suffice to say, that, for his information, he is indebted to the following sources, but chiefly to the first five, viz: Col. Stuart, Doddridge, Withers, McKiernan, DeHass, Jefferson, Howe, Dr. Knight, Felix Renick, and others.

J. H. M., 2207 Chaplin Street, Wheeling, W. Va.

THE BATTLE OF POINT PLEASANT
Dunmore's Treaty - Murder of Cornstalk.

The Battle of Point Pleasant took place in Dunmore's War, October 10th, 1774. It was the bloodiest battle perhaps ever fought with the Indians in Virginia. It had its origin in a variety of causes, but the immediate exciting cause, and that which more than all others hastened the crisis, undoubtedly was the murder of the family of Logan by the whites at or near the mouth of Yellow Creek. This disgraceful act is, by some, imputed to Colonel Cresap, a distinguished frontiersman, who resided near the town of Wheeling. Logan at least believed him to be the guilty party. By others it is strongly denied that Colonel Cresap was a participant in the affair. But, be this as it may, the act in addition to other exasperations had greatly incensed the Indian tribes on the North of the Ohio river.

The most powerful of these tribes were the Shawnee, Delaware, Mingo, Wyandotte, and Cayuga, at the head of whom was Cornstalk, Sachem of the Shawnees, and King of the Northern Confederacy. Under this renowned chieftain were other chiefs whose names were not unknown to fame; such as Redhawk, a Delaware chief; Scoppathus, a Mingo; Elinipsico, a Shawnee and a son of Cornstalk; Chiyawee, a Wyandotte; and Logan, a Cayuga, but generally spoken of as a Mingo.

To protect the settlements bordering on the Upper Ohio, it soon became necessary to organize an army in the East sufficient to operate against the savages. The effort to do this proved successful, and two bodies numbering in all twenty five hundred men were collected.

The army destined for the expedition was composed of volunteers and militia, chiefly from the counties west of the Blue Ridge, and consisted of two divisions. The northern division; comprehending the troops collected in Frederick, Dunmore (now Shenandoah) and the adjacent Counties, was to be commanded by Lord Dunmore in person; and the southern, comprising the different companies raised in Bottetourt, Augusta, and the adjoining counties east of the Blue Ridge, was to be led on by General Andrew Lewis. These two divisions proceeding by different routes were to form a junction at the mouth of the Big Kanawha, and from thence penetrate the country northwest of the Ohio river as far as the season would permit, and destroy all the Indian towns and villages they could reach. (See Appendix A for geographical information)

About the 1st of September, the troops placed under the command of General Lewis rendezvoused at Camp Union (Lewisburg) and consisted of two regiments commanded by Colonel William Fleming of Bottetourt, and Colonel Charles Lewis (brother of General Lewis) of Augusta, containing about four hundred men each. At Camp Union they were joined by an Independent volunteer company under Colonel Field of Culpeper; a company from Bedford under Captain Buford, and two from Holstein Settlement (now Washington county) under Captains' Evans, Shelby and Herbert. These three latter companies were part of the forces to be led on by Colonel Christian, who was likewise to join the two main divisions

3

of the army at Point Pleasant as soon as the other companies could be assembled. The force under General Lewis, having been thus augmented to eleven hundred men, commenced its march for the mouth of the Kanawha on the 11th of September, 1774.

From Camp Union to the point proposed for the junction of the northern and southern divisions of the army, a distance of one hundred and sixty miles, the intermediate country was a trackless forest, so rugged and mountainous as to render the progress of the army at once tedious and laborious. Under the guidance of Captain Matthew Arbuckle, they however succeeded in reaching the Ohio river after a march of nineteen days, and fixed their encampment on the point of land immediately between that river and the Big Kanawha. The provisions and ammunition transported on pack mules, and the beeves and droves arrived soon after.

When the southern division arrived at Point Pleasant, Governor Dunmore with the forces under his command had not reached there; and unable to account for his failure to form the preconcerted junction at that place, it was deemed advisable to await that event, and by so doing a better opportunity would be afforded to Colonel Christian of coming up with that portion of the army which was then with him. Meanwhile General Lewis, to learn the cause of the delay of northern division, dispatched runners by land in the direction of Fort Pitt to obtain tidings of Lord Dunmore and to communicate them to him immediately. In their absence, however, advices were received from his lordship that he had determined on proceeding across the country directly to the Shawnee towns, (on the Scioto river, about eighty miles N. W. of Point Pleasant) and ordering General Lewis to cross the river, march forward and form a junction with him near to them. These advices were received on the 9th of October, and preparations were immediately commenced for the transportation of the troops over the Ohio river.

Early on the morning of Monday, the 10th of that month, two soldiers left the camp and proceeded up the Ohio river in quest of deer. When they progressed about two miles, they unexpectedly came in sight of a large number of Indians rising from their encampment, and who, discovering the hunters, fired upon them and killed one; the other escaped unhurt, and, running briskly to the camp communicated the intelligence "that he had seen a body of the enemy covering four acres of ground as closely as they could stand by the side of each other." The main part of the army was immediately ordered out under Colonel Lewis and William Fleming, and having formed into two lines, they proceeded about four hundred yards when they met the Indians and the action commenced.

At the first onset, Colonel Charles Lewis having fallen and Colonel Fleming being wounded both lines gave way, and were retreating briskly toward the camp when they were met by a reinforcement under Colonel Field, and rallied. The engagement then became general, and was sustained by the most obstinate fury on both sides. The Indians, perceiving that the "tug of war" had come, and determined on affording the colonial army no chance of escape if victory should declare for them, formed a line extending across the point from the Ohio to the Kanawha, and protected in front by logs and fallen timber. In this situation they maintained the contest with unabated vigor from sunrise till toward the close of evening, bravely and successfully resisting every charge which was made on them, and withstanding the impetuosity of every onset with the most invincible firmness, until a fortunate movement on the part of the Virginia troops decided the day.

Some short distance above the entrance of the Kanawha river into the Ohio there is a stream called Crooked Creek, emptying into the former of these from the northeast, whose banks are tolerably high, and were then covered with a thick and luxuriant growth of weeds. Seeing the impracticability of dislodging the Indians by the most vigorous attack, and sensible of the great danger which must arise to his army if the contest were not decided before night, General Lewis detached the three companies which were commanded by Captains Isaac Shelby, George Mathews and John Stewart, with orders to proceed up the Kanawha river and Crooked creek, under cover of the banks and weeds, till they could pass some distance beyond the enemy, when they were to emerge from their covert march downward toward the point, and attack the Indians in the rear. The manoeuvre thus planned was promptly executed, and gave a decided victory to the colonial army. The Indians finding themselves suddenly and unexpectedly encompassed between two armies, and not doubting but in the rear was the looked for reinforcements under Colonel Christian, soon gave way, and about sundown commenced a precipitate retreat across the Ohio to the towns on the Scioto.

The victory indeed was decisive, and many advantages were obtained by it, but they were not cheaply bought. The Virginia army sustained in this engagement a loss of seventy five killed, and one hundred and forty wounded, about one fifth of the entire number of troops.

Among the slain were Colonels Lewis and Field, Captains Buford, Morrow, Wood, Cundiff, Wilson, and Robert McClanahan; and Lieutenants Allen, Golsby and Dillon, with some other subalterns. The loss of the enemy could not be ascertained. On the morning after the action, Colonel Christian, who had arrived after the battle ended, marched his men over the battleground and found twenty one of the Indians lying dead: and twelve others were afterwards discovered, where they had been concealed under some old logs and brush.

From the great facility with which the Indians either carry off or conceal their dead, it is always difficult to ascertain the number of their slain; and hence arises, in some measure, the disparity between their known loss and that sustained by their opponents in battle. Other reasons for this disparity are to be found in their peculiar mode of warfare and in fact that they rarely continue a contest when it has to be maintained with the loss of their warriors. It would not be easy otherwise to account for the circumstance that even when signally vanquished, the list of their slain does not frequently appear more than half as great as that of their victors. In this particular instance many of the dead were certainly thrown into the river.

Nor could the number of the enemy engaged be ever ascertained. Their army is known to have been composed of warriors from the different nations north of the Ohio, and to have composed the flower of the tribes already mentioned. The distinguished chief and consummate warrior, Cornstalk, who commanded their forces, proved himself on that day to be justly entitled to the prominent station which he occupied. His plan of alternate retreat and attack was well conceived, and occasioned the principal loss sustained by the whites. If at any time his warriors were believed to waver, his voice could be heard above the din of arms, exclaiming in his native tongue: "Be strong! Be strong!" and when one near him, by trepidation and reluctance to proceed to the charge evinced a dastardly disposition, fearing the example might have a pernicious influence, with one blow of the tomahawk he severed his skull. It was perhaps a solitary instance in which terror predominated. Never did men exhibit a more conclusive evidence of bravery in making a charge, and fortitude in withstanding an onset, than did those undisciplined soldiers of the forest in the field at Point Pleasant. Such, too, was the good conduct of those who composed the army of Virginia on that occasion, and such the noble bravery of the many, that high expectations were entertained of their future distinction. Nor were those expectations disappointed. In the various scenes through which they subsequently passed, the pledge of eminence then given was fully redeemed, and the names of Shelby, Campbell, Mathews, Fleming, Moore and others, their compatriots in arms on the memorable 10th of October, 1774, have been inscribed in brilliant characters on the roll of fame.

Having buried the dead, and made every arrangement of which their situation admitted for the comfort of the wounded, intrenchments were thrown up and the army commenced its march to form a junction with the northern division under Lord Dunmore. Proceeding by the way of the Salt Licks, General Lewis pressed forward with astonishing rapidity, (considering that the march was through a trackless desert), but before he had gone far, an express arrived from Dunmore with orders to return immediately to the mouth of the Big Kanawha. Suspecting the integrity of his Lordship's motives, and urged by the advice of his officers generally, General Lewis refused to obey these orders, and continued to advance till he was met at Kilkenny creek, and in sight of an Indian village which its inhabitants had just fired and deserted, by the Governor, accompanied by White Eyes, who in formed him that he was negotiating a treaty of peace, which would supercede the necessity of any further movement of the southern division, and repeated the order for his return.

The army under General Lewis had endured many privations, and suffered many hardships. They had encountered a savage enemy in great force, and purchased a victory with the blood of their friends. When they arrived near the goal of their anxious wishes, and with nothing to prevent the accomplishment of the object of their campaign, which was to inflict summary chastisement on the Indian tribes, they received those orders with evident chagrin and did not obey them without murmuring. Having at his own request been introduced severally to the officers of that division, complimenting them for their gallantry and good conduct in the late engagement, and assuring them of his high esteem, Lord Dunmore returned to his camp and General Lewis commenced his retrograde movement.

On his arrival at Point Pleasant, General Lewis left a sufficient force to protect the place, and a supply of provisions for the wounded, and then led the balance of the division to the place of rendezvous (Lewisburg) and disbanded them.

Lord Dunmore, after his treaty with the Indians, returned by way of Fort Gower (mouth of the Hocking) to Virginia, many of his officers and men expressing deep dissatisfaction at the course of events before and at the treaty of Camp Charlotte. The conduct of the Governor could not well be explained by them, except by supposing him to have acted with reference to the expected contest between England and her colonies, a motive which the colonists regarded as little less than treasonable. The authority for this statement is the Ohio Historical collections, and the Annals of the West. Indeed, facts and circumstances tending to this conclusion are so clear and convincing as to leave scarcely the shadow of a doubt as to Lord Dunmore's duplicity and treachery in this matter.

LORD DUNMORE'S TREATY WITH THE INDIANS.

Cornstalk had from the first opposed the war with the whites, and when his scouts reported the advance of General Lewis' division, the sagacious chief did all he could to restrain his men and keep them from battle. But all his remonstrances were in vain, and it was then he told them, "As you are determined to fight, you shall fight." After their defeat and return home, a council was convened to determine upon what was next to be done. The stern old chief said rising, "What shall we do now? The long knives are coming upon us by two routes. Shall we turn out and fight them?" "Shall we kill all our squaws and children and then fight until we are killed ourselves?" Still the congregated warriors were silent, and after a moment's hesitation, Cornstalk struck his tomahawk into the war post, and with compressed lips and flashing eyes gazed around the assembled group, then with great emphasis spoke, "Since you are not inclined to fight, I will go and make peace."

Lord Dunmore, on his return to Camp Charlotte, concluded a treaty with the Indians. Cornstalk was the chief speaker on the part of the Indians; he openly charged the whites with being the sole cause of the war, enumerating the many provocations which the Indians had received, and dwelling with great force and emphasis upon the diabolical murder of Logan's family. This great chief spoke in the most vehement and denunciatory style. His loud, clear voice was distinctly heard throughout the camp.

Colonel Wilson, who was present at the interview between Cornstalk and Lord Dunmore, thus speaks of the chieftain's bearing: "When he arose he was in no wise confused or daunted, but spoke in a distinct and audible voice, without stammering or repetition, and with peculiar emphasis. His looks while addressing Dunmore were truly grand and majestic, yet graceful and attractive, I have heard the first orators in Virginia, Patrick Henry and Richard Henry Lee, but never have I heard one whose powers of delivery surpassed those of Cornstalk."

But there was one who would not attend the camp of Lord Dunmore, and that was Logan. The Mingo chief felt the chill of despair at his heart; his very soul seemed frozen within him; and although he would not interpose obstacles to an amicable adjustment of existing difficulties, still he could not meet the Longknives in council as if no terrible stain of blood rested upon their hands. He remained at a distance, brooding in melancholy silence over his accumulated wrongs during most of the time his friends were negotiating. But Dunmore felt the importance of at least securing his assent; and for that purpose sent a special messenger, Colonel John Gibson, who waited upon the chief at his wigwam. The messenger in due time returned, bringing with him the celebrated speech which has given its author an immortality almost as imperishable as that of the great Athenian orator. But it is due perhaps in candor to state that the authenticity of this celebrated speech has been questioned.

The sentiments of the celebrated speech to which the above refers, may be, and perhaps ought to be, imputed to Logan; but to believe that an untutored savage should be able thus to excel in the rhetorical art, requires a credulity that does not ordinarily, at least, fall to the lot of cultivated minds. The speech was probably prepared by Colonel John Gibson, and polished either by himself or someone else skilled in the art of composition. Its authorship has been ascribed to Mr. Jefferson. But after reading the highly eulogistic terms in which that gentleman speaks of it, one could hardly suppose it to have been written by him. He says, "I may challenge the whole orations of Demosthenes and Cicero, and of any more eminent orator (if Europe has furnished a more eminent) to produce a single passage superior to it." This would be rather too much for any modest writer to say of his own performance. It may be added, that Dewitt Clinton indorsed the opinion expressed by Mr. Jefferson, as to this celebrated speech.

But that the intelligent reader may judge for himself, the speech of Logan, as found in Jefferson's Notes, is given below:

"I appeal," says he, "to any white man to say, if he ever entered Logan's cabin hungry, and he gave him not meat; if ever he came cold and naked, and he clothed him not. During the course of the last long and bloody war, Logan remained idle in his cabin and advocated peace. Such was my love for the whites, that my countrymen pointed as they passed and said, 'Logan is the friend of the white man.' I had even thought to live with you but for the injuries of one man. Colonel Cresap, the last spring, in cold blood and unprovoked, murdered all the relations of Logan, not even sparing my women and children. There runs not a drop of my blood in the veins of any living creature. This called on me for revenge. I have sought it; I have killed many; I have fully glutted my vengeance. For my country, I rejoice at the beams of peace, but do not harbor the thought that mine is the joy of fear. Logan never felt fear. He will not turn on his heel to save his life. Who is there to mourn for Logan? Not one."

"The Mingoes," as appears from the American Archives, "were not parties to the peace of Fort Charlotte;" but became active participants in the bloody scenes which took place when the Indians were employed as allies by the British, after the breaking out of the Revolutionary war. How far Logan himself was a participant in those scenes we do not recollect to have learned; but there can be but little doubt that he continued his hostility to the whites to the day of his death, the manner and time of which is here given:

Henry C. Brish, Esq., who derived the circumstances from Good Hunter, an aged Mingo chief, and a familiar acquaintance of Logan, says: "The last years of Logan were truly melancholy. He wandered about from tribe to tribe, a solitary and lonely man, dejected and broken hearted by the loss of his friends and the decay of his tribe. He resorted to the stimulus of strong drink to drown his sorrow. He was at last murdered in Michigan, near Detroit. He was at the time sitting with his blanket over his head before a camp fire, his elbows resting on his knees and his head upon his hands, buried in deep thought, when an Indian, who had taken some offense, stole behind him and buried his tomahawk in his brains. Thus perished the immortal Logan the last of his race." This letter of Mr. Brish is found in the Ohio Hist. Collections.

THE MURDER OF CORNSTALK.

In the year 1777 the Indians, being urged by British agents, became very troublesome to the frontier settlements, manifesting much appearance of hostility, when Cornstalk, the warrior, with Redhawk, paid a visit to the garrison at Point Pleasant. He made no secret of the disposition of the Indians, declaring that on his part he was opposed to joining in the war on the side of the British, but that all the nations except himself and his own tribe were determined to engage in it, and that of course he and his tribe would have to run with the stream.

On this Captain Arbuckle thought proper to detain him, Redhawk, and another fellow as hostages, to prevent the nation from joining the British.

In the course of that summer our Government had ordered an army to be raised, of volunteers, to serve under the command of Gen. Hand, who was to have collected a number of troops at Fort Pitt, with them descend the river to Point Pleasant, there to meet a reinforcement of volunteers expected to be raised in Augusta and Botetourt counties, and then proceed to the Shawnee towns and chastise them, so as to compel them to neutrality. Hand did not succeed in the collection of troops at Fort Pitt, and but three or four companies were raised in Augusta and Botetourt, which were under the command of Colonel George Skillern, who ordered me (Stuart) "to use my endeavors to raise all the volunteers I could in Greenbrier for that service." The people had begun to see the difficulties attending on a state of war, and long campaigns carried through wildernesses, and but a few were willing to engage in such service. But as the settlements which we covered, though less expcsed to the depredations of the Indians, had showed their willingness to aid in the proposed plan to chastise the Indians, and had raised three companies, I was very desirous of doing all I could to promote the business and aid the service. I used the utmost endeavors, and proposed to the militia officers to volunteer ourselves, which would be an encouragement to others, and by such means to raise all the men who could be got. The chief of the officers in Greenbrier agreed to the proposal, and we cast lots who should command the company. The lot fell on Andrew Hamilton for captain, and William Renick lieutenant. We collected in all about forty, and joined Colonel Skillern's party on their way to Point Pleasant.

When we arrived there was no account of General Hand or his army, and little or no provision made to support our troops other than what we had taken with us down the Kanawha.

We found too that the garrison was unable to spare us any supplies, but we concluded to wait as long as we could for the arrival of General Hand or some account of him. During our stay two young men by the names of Hamilton and Gilmore went over the Kanawha one day to hunt for deer. On their return to camp, some Indians had concealed themselves on the bank among some weeds to view our encampment, and as Gilmore came along past them, they fired on him and killed him on the bank.

Captain Arbuckle and myself were standing on the opposite bank when the gun fired, and while we were considering who it could be shooting contrary to orders, or what they were doing over the river, we saw Hamilton run down the bank, who called out that Gilmore was killed. Gilmore was one of the company of Captain John Hall, of that part of the country now Rockbridge county. The Captain was a relation of Gilmore, whose family and friends were nearly all killed by the Indians in the year 1763, when Greenbrier was cut off. Hall's men instantly jumped into a canoe and went to the relief of Hamilton, who was standing in momentary expectation of being put to death. They brought the corpse of Gilmore down the bank, covered with blood and scalped, and put him into the canoe. As they were passing the river, I observed to Captain Arbuckle that the people would be for killing the hostages as soon as the canoe should land. He supposed they would not offer to commit so great a violence upon the innocent who were in no wise accessory to the murder of Gilmore. But the canoe had hardly touched the shore until the cry was raised, 'Let us kill the Indians in the fort,' and every man, with gun in hand, came up the bank full of rage. Captain Hall was at their head and led them. Captain Arbuckle and I met them and endeavored to dissuade them from so unjustifiable an action; but they cocked their guns, threatened us with instant death if we did not desist, rushed by us into the fort, and put the Indians to death.

On the preceding day, Cornstalk's son, Elinipsico, had come from the nation to see his father, and to know if he was well or alive. When he came to the river opposite the fort he hallooed. His father was at that instant in the act of delineating, at our request, with chalk on the floor, a map of the country and the waters between the Shawnee towns and the Mississippi. He immediately recognized the voice of his son, got up, went out, and answered him. The young fellow crossed over, and they embraced each other in the most tender and affectionate manner. The interpreter's wife who had been a prisoner among the Indians and had recently left them, on hearing the uproar the next day, and hearing the men threatening that they would kill the Indians for whom she retained much affection, ran to their cabin and informed them that the people were just coming to kill them; and that, because the Indians who killed Gilmore had come with Elinipsico the day before. He utterly denied it, declaring that he knew nothing of them, and trembling exceedingly. His father encouraged him not to be afraid, for that the Great Man above had sent him there to be killed and die with him. As the men advanced to the door Cornstalk rose up and met them. They fired upon him, and seven or eight bullets went through him. So fell Cornstalk, the great warrior, whose name was bestowed upon him by the consent of the nation as their great strength and support. His son was shot dead as he sat upon a stool. Redhawk made an attempt to go up the chimney, but was shot down. The other Indian was shamefully mangled, and I grieved to see him so long in the agonies of death.

Cornstalk from personal appearance and many brave acts was undoubtedly a hero. Had he been spared to live, I believe he would have been friendly to the American cause; for nothing could have induced hint to make his visit to the garrison at the critical time he did, but to communicate to them the temper and disposition of the Indians, and their design of taking part with the British. On the day he was killed we held a council at which he was present. His countenance was dejected, and he made a speech, all of which seemed to indicate an honest and manly disposition. He seemed to be impressed with an awful premonition of his approaching fate, for he repeatedly said: 'When I was a young man and went to war, I thought that might be the last time, and I would return no more. Now I am here among you. You may kill me if you please. I can die but once, and it is all one to me, now or another time.' This declaration concluded every sentence of his speech. He was killed about one hour after the council.

The murder of Cornstalk and his party, of course, produced its natural effect, deciding the wavering Shawnees to join the other tribes as allies of the British, and converting them as possible friends of the American cause into the most bitter and relentless enemies.

THE SIEGE OF FORT HENRY.

The most important event in the history of Wheeling was the siege of Fort Henry near the mouth of Wheeling creek, in September, 1782. The bravery and perseverance of the little band who defended it against more than thirty times their number of savages, led on by the notorious Simon Girty, (see appendix B) was such as to rank it among the most memorable events in border warfare.

Fort Henry stood immediately on the east bank of the Ohio river, about a quarter of a mile above Wheeling creek. The savages, variously estimated at three hundred and eighty to five hundred warriors, having been abundantly supplied with arms and provisions by the British Governor (Hamilton) at Detroit, and led on by Simon Girty, were brought to the walls of Fort Henry before Colonel Shepherd, the commandant, knew of their real design. Some symptoms of their proximity having been discovered, the settlers of the vicinity had the night previous sought shelter within the fort.

The garrison numbered only forty two fighting men, all told, counting those advanced in years as well as those who were mere boys. A portion of them were skilled in Indian warfare and all were excellent marksmen. The storehouse was amply supplied with muskets, but was sadly deficient in ammunition.

The next morning Colonel Shepherd dispatched a man accompanied by a negro on an errand a short distance from the fort. The white man fell by a blow from the firelock of an Indian; but the negro escaped back to the fort and gave information that they had been waylaid by a party of Indians in a cornfield.

As soon as the negro related his story, the Colonel dispatched Captain Samuel Mason, with fourteen men, to dislodge the Indians from the field. Captain Mason with his party marched through the field and arrived almost on the bank of the creek without finding the Indians, and had already commenced a retrograde movement when he was suddenly and furiously assailed in front, flank and rear by the whole of Girty's army. The Captain rallied his men from the confusion produced by this unexpected demonstration of the enemy, and instantly comprehending the situation in which he was placed, gallantly took the lead and hewed a passage through the savage phalanx that opposed him. In this desperate conflict more than half the little band were slain and their leader severely wounded. Intent on retreating back to the fort, Mason pressed rapidly on with the remnant of his command, the Indians following closely in pursuit. One by one these devoted soldiers fell at the crack of the enemy's rifle. An Indian, who pursued Captain Mason, at length overtook him, and to make sure of his prey fired at him from the distance of five paces, but the shot, though it took effect, did not disable the Captain, who immediately turned about and hurling his gun at the head of his pursuer felled him to the earth. The fearlessness with which this act was performed caused an involuntary dispersion of the gang of Indians who led the pursuit; and Mason, whose extreme exhaustion of physical powers prevented him from reaching the fort, was fortunate enough to hide himself in a pile of fallen timber where he was compelled to remain to the end of the siege. Only two of his men survived the skirmish, and they, like their leader, owed their safety to the heaps of logs and brush that abounded in the cornfield

As soon as the critical situation of Captain Mason became known at the fort, Captain Ogle with twelve volunteers from the garrison, sallied forth to cover his retreat. This noble, self devoted band, in their eagerness to press forward to the relief of their suffering fellow soldiers fell into an ambuscade, and two thirds of their number were slain upon the spot. Sergeant Jacob Ogle though mortally wounded managed to escape with two soldiers into the woods, while Captain Ogle escaped in another direction and found a place of concealment, which like his brother officer, Captain Mason, he was obliged to keep as long as the siege continued. Immediately after the departure of Captain Ogle's command three new volunteers left the garrison to overtake and reinforce him. These men, however, did not reach the cornfield until after the bloody scenes had been enacted, and barely found time to return to the fort before the Indian host appeared before it. The enemy advanced in two ranks, in open order, their left flank reaching to the river bank and their right extending into the woods as far as the eye could reach. As the three volunteers were about to enter the gate a few random shots were fired at them, and instantly a loud whoop was heard on the enemy's left flank, which passed as if by concert along the line of the extreme right, until the welkin was filled with a chorus of the most wild and startling character. This salute was responded to by a few well directed rifle shots from the lower block houses, which produced a manifest confusion in the ranks of the besiegers. They discontinued their shooting and retired a few paces, probably to await the corning up of their right flank, which it would seem had been directed to make a general sweep of the bottom and then approach the stockade on the eastern side.

At this moment the garrison of Fort Henry numbered no more than twelve men and boys. The fortunes of the day so far had been fearfully against them; two of their best officers and more than two thirds of their original force were missing. The exact fate of their comrades was unknown to them, but they had every reason to apprehend that they had been cut to pieces. Still they were not dismayed; their mothers, sisters, wives and children were assembled around them; they had a sacred charge to protect, and they resolved to fight to the last extremity, and confidently trusted in Heaven for the successful issue of the combat.

When the enemy's right flank came up, Girty changed his order of attack. Parties of Indians were placed in such of the village houses as commanded a view of the blockhouses; a strong body occupied the yard of Ebenezer Zane, about fifty yards from the fort, using a paling fence as a cover, while the greater part were posted under cover in the edge of the cornfield, to act offensively or serve as a corps of reserve as occasion might require. These dispositions having been made, Girty with a white flag in his hand appeared at the window of a cabin and demanded the surrender of the garrison in the name of His Britannic Majesty. He read the proclamation of Governor Hamilton, and promised them protection if they would lay down their arms and swear allegiance to the British Crown. He warned them to submit peaceably, and admitted his inability to restrain the passions of his warriors when they once became excited with the strife of battle. Colonel Shepherd promptly told him in reply that the garrison would never surrender to him, and that he could only obtain posession of the fort when there remained no longer an American soldier to defend it. Girty renewed his proposition, but before he finished his harangue a thoughtless youth in one of the blockhouses fired a gun at the speaker and brought the conference to an abrupt termination. Girty disappeared, and in about fifteen minutes the Indians opened the seige by a general discharge of rifles.

It was yet quite early in the morning, the sun not having appeared above the summit of Wheeling hill, and the day is represented as being one of surpassing beauty. The Indians, not entirely concealed from the view of the garrison, kept up a brisk fire for the space of six hours without much intermission. The little garrison, in spite of its heterogeneous character, was with scarcely an exception composed of sharpshooters. Several of them whose experience in Indian warfare gave them a remarkable degree of coolness and self possession in the face of danger, infused confidence into the young, and, as they never fired at random, their bullets in most cases took effect. The Indians, on the contrary, gloated with their previous success, their tomahawks reeking with the blood of Mason's and Ogle's men, and all of them burning with impatience to rush into the fort and complete their work of butchery, discharged their guns against the pickets, the gate, the logs of the block houses, and every other object that seemed to shelter a white man. Their fire was thrown away. At length some of the most daring warriors rushed up close to the block houses, and attempted to make sure work by firing through the logs; but these reckless savages received from the well directed rifles of the frontiersmen the fearful reward of their temerity. About one o'clock the Indians discontinued their fire and fell back against the base of the hill.

The stock of gunpowder in the fort having been nearly exhausted, it was determined to seize the favorable opportunity afforded by the suspension of hostilities, to send for a keg of powder which was known to be in the house of Ebenezer Zane, about sixty yards from the gate of the fort. The person executing this service would necessarily expose himself to the danger of being shot down by the Indians, who were yet sufficiently near to observe everything that transpired about the works. The Colonel explained the matter to his men and unwilling to order one of them to undertake such a desperate enterprise, inquired whether any man would volunteer for the service.

Three or four young men promptly stepped forward in obedience to the call. The Colonel informed them that the weak state of the garrison would not justify the absence of more than one man, and it was for themselves to decide who that person should be. The eagerness felt by each volunteer to undertake the honorable mission prevented them from making the arrangement proposed by the commandant, and so much time was consumed in the contention, that fears began to arise that the Indians would renew the attack before the powder could be procured. At this crisis a young lady, the sister of Ebenezer and Silas Zane, came forward and desired that she might be permitted to execute the service. This proposition seemed so extravagant that it met with a peremptory refusal, but she instantly renewed her petition in terms of redoubled earnestness, and all the remonstrances of the Colonel and her relatives failed to dissuade her from her heroic purpose. It was finally represented to her that either of the young men, on account of his superior fleetness and familiarity with scenes of danger, would be more likely than herself to do the work successfully. She replied, that the danger which would attend the enterprise was the identical reason that induced her to offer her services, for as the garrison was very weak, no soldier's life should be placed in needless jeopardy, and that if she were to fall, her loss would not be felt. Her petition was ultimately granted, and the gate opened for her to pass out. The opening of the gate arrested the attention of several Indians who were straggling through the village. It was noticed that their eyes were upon her as she crossed the open space to reach her brother's house; but seized perhaps with a sudden freak of clemency, or believing that a woman's life was not worth a load of gunpowder, or influenced by some unexplained motive they permitted her to pass without molestation. When she reappeared with the powder in her arms, the Indians suspecting no doubt the character of her burden, elevated their firelocks and discharged a volley at her as she swiftly glided toward the gate; but the balls all flew wide of their mark, and the fearless girl reached the fort in safety with her prize. (Thus far, this narrative is substantially the same as that of McKiernan, who is supposed to have derived his information in part, at least, from Withers, the former having written in 1843, the latter in 1832.)

It is but fair, that in connection with this narrative, in regard to the powder exploit, should be read, a counter statement by Mrs. Lydia S. Cruger, which will be found in Appendix C.

About half past two o'clock the Indians put themselves again in motion, and advanced to renew the siege. As in the first attack, a portion of the warriors took possession of the cabins contiguous to the fort, while others availed themselves of the cover afforded by Zane's paling fence. A large number posted themselves in and behind a blacksmith shop and a stable that stood opposite the northern line of pickets, and another party, probably the strongest of all, stationed themselves under cover of a worm fence and several large piles of fallen timber on the south side of the fort. The siege was now reopened from the latter quarter, a strong gang of Indians advancing under cover of some large stumps that stood on the side of the declivity below the fort, and renewing the combat with loud yells and brisk fire. The impetuosity of the attack on the south side brought the whole garrison to the lower block houses, from which they were enabled to pour out a destructive fire upon the enemy in that quarter. While the garrison was thus employed, a party of eighteen or twenty Indians armed with rails and billets of wood, rushed out of Zane's yard and made an attempt to force open the gate of the fort. Their design was discovered in time to defeat it, but only abandoned after five or six of their number had been shot down. Upon the failure of this scheme, the Indians opened a fire upon the fort from all sides, except from that next to the river, which afforded no shelter to a besieging host. On the north and east the battle raged most fiercely; for notwithstanding the strength of the assailants on the south, the unfavorableness of the ground prevented them from prosecuting with much vigor the attack which they had commenced with such fury.

The rifles used by the garrison, towards evening became so much heated by continued firing that they were rendered measurably useless, and recourse was then had to muskets, a full supply of which was found in the storehouse. As darkness set in the fire of the savages grew weaker, though it was not entirely discontinued until next morning. Shortly after nightfall a considerable party of Indians advanced within sixty yards of the fort, bringing with them a hollow maple log, which they had converted into a field piece by plugging up one of its ends with a block of wood.

To give it additional strength a quantity of chains taken from the blacksmith shop, encompassed it from one end to the other. It was heavily charged with powder and then filled to the muzzle with pieces of stone, slugs of iron, and such other hard substances as could be found. The cannon was graduated carefully to discharge its contents against the gate of the fort. When the match was applied it burst into many fragments; and although it produced no effect upon the fort, it killed and wounded several of the Indians, who stood by to witness its discharge. A loud yell succeded the failure of this experiment, and the crowd dispersed. By this time the Indians had generally withdrawn from the siege and fallen back against the hill to take rest and food. Numbers of stragglers, however, lurked about the village all night, keeping up an irregular fire on the fort, and destroying whatever articles of furniture and household comfort they chanced to find in the cabins.

Late in the evening, Francis Duke, a son-in-law of Colonel Shepherd, arrived from the forks of Wheeling, and was shot down by the Indians before he could reach the gate of the fort. About four o'clock next morning, September 28th, Colonel Swearingen with fourteen men, arrived in a pirogue from Cross creek, and was fortunate enough to fight his way into the fort without the loss of a man.

About daybreak Major Samuel McColloch, with forty mounted men from Short creek, came to the relief of the little garrison. The gate was thrown open, and McColloch's men, though closely beset by the Indians, entered in safety, but McColloch himself was not permitted to pass the gateway; the Indians crowded around him and separated him from his party. After several ineffectual attempts to force his way to the gate, he wheeled about and galloped with the swiftness of a deer in the direction of Wheeling hill.

McCOLLOCH'S LEAP.

The Indian's might easily have killed him, but they charged towards him an almost frenzied hatred; for he had participated in so many encounters that almost every warrior personally knew him. To take him alive and glut their full revenge by the most fiendish tortures was their object, and they made almost superhuman exertions to capture him. He put spurs to his horse and soon became completely hemmed in on three sides, and the fourth was almost a perpendicular precipice of 150 feet descent, with Wheeling creek at its base. Supporting his rifle on his left hand, and carefully adjusting his reins with the other, he urged his horse to the brink of the bluff and then made the leap which decided his fate. In the next moment the noble steed, still bearing his intrepid rider in safety, was at the foot of the precipice. McColloch immediately dashed across the creek and was soon beyond the reach of the Indians.

After the escape of Major McColloch, the Indians concentrated at the foot of the hill and soon after set fire to all the houses and fences outside of the fort, and killed about three hundred head of cattle belonging to the settlers. They then raised the siege and took up the line of march to some other theater of action.

During the investiture, not a single man within the fort was killed, and only one wounded, and that wound was a slight one. But the loss sustained by the whites during the enemy's inroad was remarkably severe. Of the forty two men who were in the fort on the morning of the 27th, no less than twenty three were killed in the cornfield before the siege commenced. Two men who had been sent down the river the previous night in a canoe, were intercepted and killed; and if we include Duke in the list, the loss sustained by the settlement amounted to twenty six killed, besides four or five wounded. The enemy's loss was from sixty to one hundred. Agreeably to their ancient custom, they removed their dead from the field before the siege was raised; the extent of their loss, therefore, is merely conjectural.

The larger number of the Indians returned to their homes committing such depredations by the way as they could. About one hundred of them scoured the country east of Wheeling, and after murdering a number of men, women and children, made an attack on Rice's fort, and some block houses in the neighborhood, which being gallantly defended, they were compelled to withdraw. Fearing to make further delay, and scattering themselves into small bands, they recrossed the Ohio and returned to their homes. It should be added that the people in the neighborhood of Rice's fort had received short notice of the coming of the Indians, through two white men who had been their prisoners, and who had deserted them at Wheeling. Otherwise the inhabitants of that neighborhood might have been utterly destroyed.

McCOLLOCH'S DEATH.

As the reader will very naturally desire to learn the fate of Major McColloch after his almost miraculous escape from the Indians, some account of the manner of his death may be properly introduced in this place.

Not long after the siege of Fort Henry, indications of Indians having been noticed by some of the settlers, Major McColloch and his brother John mounted their horses and left Van Metre's fort to ascertain the correctness of the report. They crossed Short creek, and continued in the direction of Wheeling, but inclining towards the river. They scouted closely but cautiously, and not discovering any such "signs" as had been stated, descended to the river bottom at a point on the farm subsequently owned by Alfred P. Woods, about two miles above Wheeling. They then passed up the river to the mouth of Short creek, and thence up Girty's Point in the direction of Van Metre's. Not discovering any indications of the enemy, the brothers were riding leisurely along, and when a short distance beyond the "point" a deadly discharge of rifles took place, killing Major Samuel McColloch instantly. His brother John escaped, but his horse was killed. Immediately mounting that of his brother he made off to give the alarm. As yet no enemy had been seen; but turning in his saddle after riding fifty yards, the path was filled with Indians, and one fellow was seen in the act of scalping the unfortunate Major. Quick as thought the rifle of John was at his shoulder; an instant later, and the savage was rolling in the agonies of death. John escaped to the fort unhurt with the exception of a slight wound of his hip.

On the following day, a party of men from Van Metre's went out and gathered up the mutilated remains of Major McColloch. The savages had disembowled him, but the viscera all remained except the heart. Some years subsequent to this melancholy affair, an Indian who had been one of the party on this occasion told some whites that the heart of Major McColloch had been divided and eaten by the party. "This was done," said he, "that we be bold like Major McColloch." On another occasion, an Indian in speaking of the incident said, "The whites (meaning John McColloch) had killed a great captain; but they (the Indians) had killed a greater one."

The question has been mooted whether Samuel McColloch or his younger brother John, of whom honorable mention has just been made, was the real hero of the "leap;" but this point has been so thoroughly sifted, that there no longer remains the shadow of doubt that Samuel McColloch was the identical person; so that the subject may be safely dismissed as not requiring further discussion.

CAPTAIN FOREMAN AND MEN.

About four miles above the present town of Moundsville, on the Ohio river, is a monument bearing the following inscription:

"This humble stone is erected to the, memory of Captain Foreman and twenty one of his men, who were slain by a band of ruthless savages, the allies of a civilized nation of Europe, on the 25th of September, 1777."

> "So sleep the brave who sink to rest,
> By all their country's wishes blest."

Captain William Foreman, a brave and meritorious officer, but unskilled, it should be said, in Indian warfare, organized a volunteer company in Hampshire county, Virginia, and marched to Wheeling in the fall of 1777. On Sunday morning, September 24th, a smoke was "noticed by some person at Wheeling, in the direction of Grave creek, which caused an apprehension that the Indians might be burning the stockade and houses of Mr. Tomlinson. In order to ascertain the fact and afford protection, if any were necessary, Captain Foreman, with his company and a few experienced scouts, were dispatched by Colonel Shepherd for that purpose.

The party proceeded without interruption to Grave creek and found all safe. Remaining over night they started the following morning to return. When they reached the lower end of the narrows, some of the more experienced frontier men suggested the expediency of leaving the river bottom and returning by way of the ridge. The commander, however, hooted at the idea of so much caution and ordered the party to proceed. The order was obeyed by his own men, including several of the scouts; but some declined to go with him, and of these was a man named Lynn, whose great experience as a spy, added to his sagacity and judgment, should at least have rendered his opinions valuable and entitled to weight. His apprehensions were that the Indians, if lurking about, had watched the movements of the party and would most likely attack them at some point on the river. He said, that in all probability, they had been on the opposite side of the river and noticed the party go down; that they had crossed during the night, and probably were at that time lying in ambush for their return.

During the interchange of opinions between Foreman and Lynn, the controversy at times ran high. Foreman, who prided himself on being a thoroughly disciplined officer, was not disposed to yield to the suggestions of a rough backwoodsman. Lynn, on the other hand, convinced of the fatal error which the other seemed determined to commit, could not but remonstrate with great earnestness. Finally, when the order to march was given, Lynn with some six or eight others struck up the hillside, while Foreman with his company pursued the path along the base. Nothing of importance occurred until the party reached the extreme upper end of the narrows. Just where the bottom begins to widen, those in front had their attention called to a display of Indian trinkets, beads, bands, etc., strewn in profusion along the path. With a natural curiosity, but with a great lack of caution, the entire party gathered about those who picked up the articles of decoy, and whilst thus standing in a group looking at the trinkets, two lines of Indians stretched across the path, one above, the other below, and a large body of them simultaneously arose from beneath the bank and opened upon the devoted party a most deadly and destructive fire. The hill rises at this point very abruptly, presenting an almost insurmountable barrier. Still, those of the party who escaped the first discharge attempted to rush up the hill, and some with success. But the savages pursued and killed several.

At the first fire Captain Foreman and most of his party, including his two sons, fell dead. The exact loss cannot with certainty be ascertained, but it is supposed to have been about twenty, including the Captain

When Lynn and his party heard the guns they rushed down the hillside, hallooing as though they were five times as numerous. This had the effect of restraining the savages in pursuit. Of those who escaped up the hill were Robert Harkness and John Collins. The former in pulling himself up by a sapling had the bark knocked into his face by a ball from an Indian's gun. Collins was shot through the left thigh, breaking the bone and completely disabling him. Lynn and his companions carried him to a spring, supposed to be the one near the present residence of Colonel Samuel Baker, and throwing together their supply of provisions, left him in a sheltered position, promising to send a horse for him the next day, which was accordingly done. Collins recovered and lived for many years.

On the second day a party went down and buried the dead. Colonel Shepherd, Colonel Zane, Andrew Poe and Martin Wetzel were of the number. The slain were buried in one common grave, and the site is indicated by the stone already described. (This stone has recently been removed to the town of Moundsville, with ceremonies; but why should it not have been left to indicate the spot where the fatal disaster occurred?)

THE MORAVIAN MASSACRE.

The Moravian Indians consisted chiefly of Delawares and Mohicans, who had been converted to Christianity through the zeal and influence of the Moravian missionaries. They had four towns on the Upper Muskingum, in the line of travel between the nearest point on the Ohio river and Upper Sandusky, the home of the Delawares and other warlike tribes. The Moravian Indians were always friendly toward the whites. During the whole of the Revolutionary war they had remained neutral, or if they took part, it was in favor of the Americans, advising them of the approach of hostile Indians and rendering other kindly offices. For ten years of border strife they had lived in peace and quietness, but at length became objects of suspicion to both whites and savages. They were, it may be said, between two fires. While passing to and fro, the hostile parties would compel them to furnish provisions. It is not surprising, therefore, that they should have fallen a sacrifice to one or the other.

It happened that early in February, 1782, a party of Indians from Sandusky penetrated the white settlements and committed numerous depredations. Of the families which fell beneath the murderous stroke of these savages was that of David Wallace, consisting of himself, wife and six children, and at the same time a man named Carpenter was taken prisoner. The early date of this visitation induced the whites to believe that the depredators had wintered with the Moravians, and they at once resolved on executing summary vengeance. About the first of March, a body of eighty or ninety men rendezvoused at Mingo Bottom, a few miles below the present town of Steubenville, Ohio. The second day's march brought them within a short distance of one of the Moravian towns, of which there were four, and they encamped for the night.

The victims received warning of their danger, but took no measures to escape believing that they had nothing to fear from the Americans. On the arrival of an advanced party of sixteen men, they professed peace and good will to the Moravians, and informed them that they had come to take them to Fort Pitt for safety. The Indians surrendered, delivering up their arms, even their hatchets, on being promised that everything should he restored to them on their arrival at Pittsburgh. By persuasion of some and driving of others, the inhabitants of two or three of the towns had been brought together and bound without resistance. A council of war was then held to decide their fate. The commandant, Colonel David Williamson, at the suggestion of his officers, then put the question to his men in form, "Whether the Moravian Indians should be taken prisoners to Pittsburgh or put to death?" and requested that all who were in favor of saving their lives should step out of the line and form a second rank. On this sixteen men stepped out and formed themselves into a second line. The fearful determination of putting the Moravians to death was thus shown.

Most of those opposed to this diabolical resolution, protested in the name of high heaven against the atrocious act, and called God to witness that they were innocent of the blood of these people; yet the majority remained unmoved, and some of them were even in favor of burning them alive. But it was at length decided that they should be scalped in cold blood, and the Indians were told to prepare for their fate. They were led into buildings, in one of which the men, and in the other the women and children, were confined like sheep for the slaughter. They passed the night in praying and exhorting one another, and singing hymns of praise to God.

When the morning arrived, for the purpose of slaughter, two houses were selected, one for the men, and the other for the women and children: The victims were then bound two and two together, led into the slaughter houses, and there scalped and murdered. The number of the slain, according to the Moravian account, for many of them had made their escape, was ninety six. Of these, sixty two were grown persons, one third of whom were women; the remaining thirty four were children.

After the work of death had been finished and the plunder secured, all the buildings in the towns were set on fire. A rapid retreat to the settlements concluded this deplorable campaign. (see Appendix D)

"In justice to the memory of Colonel Williamson," says Doddridge, "I have to say, that although at that time very young, I was personally acquainted with him, and from my recollection of his conversation, I say with confidence that he was a brave man, but not cruel. He would meet an enemy in battle and fight like a soldier, but not murder a prisoner. Had he possessed the authority of a superior officer in a regular army, I do not believe that a single Moravian Indian would have lost his life; but he possessed no such authority. He was only a militia officer, who could advise but not command.

41

His only fault was that of too easy compliance with popular opinion and popular prejudice. On this account his memory has been loaded with unmerited reproach.

"Should it be asked what sort of people composed this band of murderers, I answer, they were not all miscreants or vagabonds; many of them were men of the first standing in the country. Many of them had recently lost relations by the hands of the savage, and were burning with revenge. They cared little on whom they wreaked their vengeance, so they were Indians."

"When attacked by our people, although the Moravians might have defended themselves, they did not. They never fired a single shot. They were prisoners, and had been promised protection. Every dictate of justice required that their lives should be spared. It was, therefore, an atrocious and unqualified murder."

The fate of the Moravians was probably decided by a mob, which Colonel Williamson felt himself powerless to control, in which a few infuriated spirits, by clamor, violence and intimidation of weaker minds, carried them forward against their own convictions to the perpetration of this diabolical wickedness. In such a crisis, as it seems to the writer, even hesitation is a crime; and though he is prepared to sympathize with Colonel Williamson to the extent of pitying his embarrassment, he is not disposed to exonerate him from severe censure. In such a case, it would have been better for his reputation had he thrown himself into the breach and died in the struggle, rather than allow such a gross triumph of wicked barbarity over the acknowledged principles of justice and humanity. Had he done this at the critical moment, perhaps the majority would have sprung to his side, and thus this burning and cruel shame might have been avoided.

Every person knows what one bold and determined spirit in a crisis like this can accomplish, and what responsive throbs such heroic deeds awaken in the hearts of all true lovers of humanity. But still, all men are not capable of all things, and the Moravian massacre will forever remain a foul blot upon the historic page.

CRAWFORD'S CAMPAIGN.

The object of this campaign was twofold: First, to complete the work of murdering and plundering the Moravians at their new establishment on the Sandusky; and secondly, to destroy the Wyandotte towns on the same river. It was the resolution of all concerned in this expedition not to spare the life of any Indian that might fall into their hands, friend or foe, man, woman or child. But as will be seen in the sequel, the result was widely different from that of the Moravian campaign of the preceding March.

It would seem that the long continuance of this Indian war had greatly demoralized the early settlers, and being prompted by an indiscriminate thirst for revenge, they were prepared to go to almost any extreme of barbarity.

On the 25th of May, 1782, four hundred and eighty men mustered at Mingo Bottom and proceeded to elect their commander. The choice fell upon Colonel William Crawford, who accepted the command with some degree of reluctance.

The army marched along "Williamson's trail" until they arrived at the ruins of the upper Moravian town, in the fields belonging to which there was still plenty of corn on the stalks, with which their horses were fed during the night.

Shortly after the army halted at this place, two Indians were discovered by some men who had walked out of the camp. Three shots were fired at one of them, but without effect. As soon as the news reached the camp, more than one half of the men rushed out, without command, and in the most tumultuous manner, to see what had happened. From that time Colonel Crawford felt a presentiment of the defeat which followed.

The truth is, that notwithstanding the secrecy and dispatch with which the enterprise had been gotten up, the Indians were beforehand with the whites. They saw the rendezvous on the Mingo Bottom, and knew the number and destination of the troops. They visited every encampment immediately after the troops had left, and saw from their writing on the trees and scraps of paper, that "no quarter" was to be given to any Indian, whether man, woman or child.

Nothing of importance happened during their march until the 6th of June, when their guide conducted them to the site of the Moravian villages on one of the upper branches of the Sandusky river. From this retreat the Christian Indians had lately been driven away by the Wyandottes to the Scioto, and here the army of Colonel Crawford, instead of finding Indians and plunder, met with nothing but vestiges of ruin and desolation.

In this dilema what was to be done? The officers held a council, in which it was determined to march one day longer in the direction of Upper Sandusky, and if they should not reach the town in the course of a day, to make a retreat with all possible speed.

The march was commenced the next morning through the plains of Sandusky, and continued until 2 o'clock, when the advance guard was attacked and driven in by the Indians, who were discovered in large numbers in the high grass with which the place was covered.

The Indian army was at that moment about entering a large piece of wood almost entirely surrounded by plains; but in this they were disappointed by a rapid movement of the whites. The battle then commenced by a heavy fire from both sides. From a partial possession of the woods, which they had gained at the outset of the battle, the Indians were soon dislodged. They then attempted to gain a small skirt of wood on the right flank of Colonel Crawford, but were prevented from so doing by the vigilance and bravery of Major Leet, who at the time commanded the right wing. The firing was heavy and incessant until dark, when it ceased, and both armies lay on their arms during the night. Both adopted the policy of kindling large fires along the line of battle, and then retiring some distance in the rear of them to prevent being surprised by a night attack. During the conflict of the afternoon, three of our men were killed and several wounded.

In the morning, Colonel Crawford's army occupied the battleground of the preceding day. The Indians made no attack during the day until late in the evening, but were seen in large bodies traversing the plains in various directions. Some of them appeared to be carrying off the dead and wounded.

In the morning of this day a council of officers was held, and a retreat was resolved on as the only means of saving the army, the Indians appearing to increase in numbers every hour.

During the day, preparations were made for a retreat by burying the dead, burning fires over the graves to prevent discovery, and preparing means for carrying off the wounded. The retreat was to commence in the course of the night. The Indians however, became apprised of the intended retreat, and about sundown attacked the army with great force and fury, in every direction except that of Sandusky. When the line of march was formed and the retreat commenced, Colonel Crawford's guides prudently took the direction of Sandusky, which afforded the only opening in the Indian lines and the only chance of concealment. After marching about a mile in this direction the army wheeled about to the left, and by a circuitous route, gained before day the trail by which they came. They continued their march the whole of the next day, without further annoyance than the firing of a few distant shots by the Indians at the rear guard, which slightly wounded two or three men. At night they built fires, took their suppers, secured the horses, and resigned themselves to repose without placing a single sentinel or vidette for safety. In this careless situation they might have been surprised and cut off by the Indians, who however did not disturb them during the night, nor afterwards during the whole retreat. The number that retreated in the main body is supposed to have been about three hundred.

But several parties supposing that they could more effectually secure their safety, by breaking off from the main army in small numbers, were pursued by the Indians and nearly all of them slain.

At the commencement of the retreat Colonel Crawford placed himself at the head of the army, and continued there until they had gone about a quarter of a mile, when missing his son, John Crawford, his son-in-law, Major Harrison, and his nephews, Major

Rose and William Crawford, he halted and called for them as the line passed, but without finding them. After the army had passed him he was unable to overtake it, owing to the weariness of his horse. Falling in company with Dr. Knight and two others, they traveled all night, first north, and then to the east, to avoid the pursuit of the Indians. They directed their courses by the north star.

On the next day, they fell in with Captain John Biggs and Lieutenant Ashley, the latter of whom was wounded. Two others were in company with Biggs and Ashley. They encamped together the succeeding night. On the next day, while on their march, they were attacked by a party of Indians, who made Colonel Crawford and Dr. Knight prisoners. The other four made their escape, but Captain Biggs and Lieutenant Ashley were killed the day following.

"The Colonel and I," says Dr. Knight, "were then taken to the Indian camp, which was about half a mile from the place where we were captured. On Sunday evening, five Delawares who had posted themselves at some distance further on the road, brought back to the camp where we lay, Captain Biggs' and Lieutenant Ashley's scalps, with an Indian scalp which Captain Biggs had taken in the field of action. They also brought in Biggs' horse and mine. They told us the two other men got away from them.

"Monday morning, the 10th of June, we were paraded to march to Sandusky, about thirty three miles distant. They had eleven prisoners of us and four scalps, the Indians being seventeen in number.

"Colonel Crawford was very desirous to see a certain Simon Girty who lived among the Indians, and was on this account permitted to go to town the same night, with two warriors to guard him, they having orders at the same time to pass by the place where the Colonel had turned out his horse, that they might if possible find him. The rest of us were taken as far as the old town (Sandusky) which was within eight miles of the new.

"Tuesday morning, the 11th, Colonel Crawford was brought out of town on purpose to be marched in with the other prisoners. I asked the Colonel if he had seen Mr. Girty. He told me he had, and that Girty had promised to do everything in his power for him, but that the Indians were very much enraged against the prisoners, particularly Captain Pipe, one of the chiefs; he likewise told me that Girty had informed him that his son-in-law, Colonel Harrison, and his nephew, William Crawford, were made prisoners by the Shawnees, but had been pardoned. This Captain Pipe had come from the towns about an hour before Colonel Crawford, and had painted all the prisoners' faces black.

"As he was painting me, he told me I should go to the Shawnee towns, and see my friends. When the Colonel arrived he painted him black also, told him he was glad to see him, and that he would have him shaved when he came to see his friends at the Wyandotte town. When we marched, the Colonel and I were kept between Pipe and Wingenim, the two Delaware chiefs, the other nine prisoners were sent forward with a party of Indians. As we went along we saw four of the prisoners lying by the path tomahawked and scalped; some of them were at the distance of half a mile from the others. When we arrived within half a mile of the place where the Colonel was executed; we overtook the five prisoners that remained alive. The Indians had caused them to sit down on the ground; also the Colonel and myself at some distance from them. I was then given in charge of an Indian fellow to be taken to the Shawnee towns.

"In the place where we were now made to sit down, there was a number of squaws and boys who fell on the five prisoners and tomahawked them. There was a certain John McKinley among the prisoners, formerly an officer in the 13th Virginia Regiment, whose head an old squaw cut off. The young Indian fellows came often where the Colonel and I were, and dashed the scalps in our faces. We were then conducted along towards the place where the Colonel was afterwards executed. When we came within a half a mile of it, Simon Girty met us, with several Indians on horseback. He spoke to the Colonel, but as I was about one hundred and fifty yards behind, I could not hear what passed between them.

"Almost every Indian we met struck us with fist or sticks. Girty waited till I was brought up, and then asked, 'Is that the doctor?' I answered, 'Yes,' and went toward him, reaching out my hand, but he bid me begone, and called me a damned rascal; upon which the fellow who had me in charge pulled me along. Girty rode up after me and told me that I was to go to the Shawnee towns.

"When we came to the fire, the Colonel was stripped naked, ordered to sit down by the fire, and then they beat him with sticks and fists. Presently after, I was treated in the same manner.

"They then tied a rope to the foot of a post about fifteen feet high, bound the Colonel's hands behind his back, and fastened the rope to the ligature between his wrists. The rope was long enough either for him to sit down or walk round the post once or twice and return the same way. The Colonel then called to Girty, and asked if they intended to burn him? Girty answered, 'Yes.' The Colonel said he would take it all patiently. Upon this, Captain Pipe, a Delaware chief, made a speech to the Indians, consisting of about thirty or forty men, and sixty or seventy squaws and boys.

"When the speech was finished, they all yelled a hideous and hearty assent to what had been said. The Indian men then took up their guns and shot powder into the Colonel's body, from his feet as far up as his neck. I think not less than seventy loads were discharged upon his naked body. They then crowded about him, and to the best of my observation, cut off his ears. When the throng had dispersed a little I saw the blood running from both sides of his head.

"The fire was about six or seven yards from the post to which the Colonel was tied; it was made of small hickory poles, burnt quite through in the middle, each end of the poles remaining about six feet in length. Three or four Indians, by turns, would take up individually one of these burning pieces of wood and apply it to his naked body, already burnt black with powder. These tormentors presented themselves on every side of him, so that whichever way he ran round the post they met him with the burning fagots and poles. Some of the squaws took broad boards, upon which they would put a quantity of burning coals and hot embers and throw them on him,

51

so that in a short time he had nothing but coals of fire and hot ashes to walk upon.

"In the midst of these extreme tortures, he called to Simon Girty, and begged him to shoot him; but Girty making no answer, he called him again. Girty then by way of derision told the Colonel he had no gun, and at the same time turning about to an Indian who was behind him, laughed heartily, and by all his gestures seemed delighted at the horrid scene.

"Girty then came up to me and bade me prepare for death. He said, however, 'I was not to die at that place, but to be burnt at the Shawnee towns. He swore by G—d I need not expect to escape death, but should suffer it in all it extremities.'

"Colonel Crawford, at this period of his suffering, besought the Almighty to have mercy on his soul, spoke very low, and bore his torments with the most manly fortitude. He continued, in all the extremities of pain, for an hour and three quarters, or two hours longer, as near as I can judge, when at last being almost spent he laid down on his belly. They then scalped him, and repeatedly threw the scalp in my face, telling me, 'That is your great Captain's'. An old squaw (whose appearance every way answered the idea people entertained of the devil) got a board and took a parcel of coals and ashes and laid them on his back and head after he had been scalped. He then raised upon his feet and began to walk round the post. They next put a burning stick to him, as usual, but he seemed more insensible to pain than before. After he expired, his body was thrown into the fire and consumed to ashes."

ESCAPE OF DR. KNIGHT.

Colonel Crawford was about fifty years of age when he suffered at the stake. His son-in-law and nephew were executed about the same time. His son John escaped. Dr. Knight was doomed to be executed, at a town about fifty miles from Sandusky, and was committed to the care of a young Indian to be taken there. The first day they traveled about twenty five miles, and encamped for the night. In the morning, the gnats being very troublesome, the Doctor requested the Indian to untie him that he might help to make a fire to keep them off. With this request the Indian complied. While the Indian was on his knees and elbows blowing the fire, the Doctor caught up a piece of tent pole which had been burned in two, about eighteen inches long, with which he struck the Indian on the head with all his might, so as to knock him forward into the fire. The stick, however, broke, so that the Indian, although severely hurt, was not killed, but immediately sprang up. On this, the Doctor caught up the Indian's gun to shoot him, but drew back the cock with so much force as to break the main spring. The Indian ran off with a hideous yell. The Doctor then made the best of his way home, which he reached in twenty one days, almost famished. On his journey he subsisted on roots and a few young birds and berries.

ESCAPE OF SLOVER.

The Grenadier Squaw, as she was called, was the sister of the great Cornstalk. She remained true to the Americans, even after the cruel murder of her brother. It seems that she had a town of her own, on the left side of the Scippo, and but a short distance southeast of her brother's town, on Pickaway Plains. It was at her town, that the captives taken to the Scioto, were compelled to run the gauntlet, and be burnt at the stake. Such an ordeal was prepared for a Mr. John Slover, who was taken prisoner at Crawford's defeat, in 1782. He was brought to Grenadier Squaw town, to suffer a similar death to that which Crawford, his commander, had undergone a few days before, but from which, through providential aid, he was relieved and enabled to make his escape.

After his capture, on his way to the Shawnee towns, he had been very much abused at the different towns he passed through, beaten with clubs, &c. On his arrival he had a similar punishment to undergo. A council was held over him, and he was doomed to die the death that Crawford had suffered. The day was appointed for the consummation of the horrid deed, and its morning dawned without any unpropitious appearances, to mar the anticipated enjoyments of the natives collected from the neighboring towns to witness the scene. At the appointed time, Slover was led forth, stripped naked, tied to the fatal stake, and the fire kindled around him. Just as the tormentors were about to commence the torture, it seemed that the

Great Spirit looked down and said, "No, this horrid deed shall not be done." Immediately the heavens were overcast; the forked lightnings in all directions flew, in mighty peals the thunder rolled, and seemed to shake the earth to its center; the rain in copious torrents fell, and quenched the threatening flames before they had done the victim much injury, continuing to a late hour. The natives stood dumfounded, somewhat fearing that the Great Spirit was not pleased with what they were about to do. But had they been ever so much inclined, there was not time left that evening to carry out their usual savage observances. Slover was, therefore, taken from the stake, and conducted to an empty house, to an upper log of which he was fastened by a buffalo tug tied around his neck, and his arms were pinioned behind him by a cord. Two warriors were set over him as a guard to prevent his escape in the night. Here Providence seemed to interfere in favor of Slover, by causing a restless sleep to come over his guard. Until a late hour, the Indians sat up smoking their pipes and talking to Slover, using all their ingenuity to tantalize him, asking "how he would like to eat fire," &c. At length one of them lay down and soon fell asleep. The other continued smoking and talking to Slover for some time. After midnight, a deep sleep came upon him, he also lay down, and soon thought of nothing, save in dreams of the anticipated pleasure to be enjoyed in torturing their prisoner next day. Slover then resolved to make an effort to get loose, and soon extricated one of his hands from the cords. He then tried to unloose the tug around his neck, but without effect. He had not long been thus engaged, before one of the Indians got up and smoked his pipe. While he was thus engaged, Slover kept very still for fear of discovery, but the Indian being overcome with sleep, again lay down. Slover then renewed his exertions, but for some time without effect, and he resigned himself to his fate. After resting awhile, however, he resolved to make another and a last effort. He put his hand again to the tug, and, as he related, he slipped it over his head without difficulty. He then got out of the house as quietly as possible, and sprang over a fence into a cornfield. While passing through the field, he came near running over a squaw and her children, who was sleeping under a tree. To avoid discovery he deviated from a straight track, and rapidly hurried to the upper plain, where, as he had expected, he found a number of Indian horses grazing. Day was then faintly breaking. He untied the cord from the other arm, which by this time was much swelled; selecting, as he thought, the best horse he could see, he made a bridle of the cord, mounted him, and rode off at full speed. About 10 o'clock the horse gave out. Slover then had to travel on foot with all possible speed, and between mosquitoes, nettles, brush, briars, thorns, etc., by the time he got home to Wheeling, he had more the appearance of a piece of raw flesh, than an animated being.

Thus ends this sad and heart rending story with its incidents; and thus it may be said were the Moravians signally avenged. But to what extent the sword of justice fell upon the real guilty parties, the writer does not pretend to know, nor does he consider it his province to decide. But to every reflective mind it must be evident, that the disasters connected with this unfortunate campaign, may be referred to in a general way, as furnishing one of the many striking proofs afforded by the history of the world, that retributive justice is sooner or later meted out to evil doers, and that "the way of the transgressor is hard," whether it be spoken of individuals or communities. Those who claim to live under the laws of civilization should not allow themselves to be governed by the rules which belong only to a state of savage lawlessness.

Having narrated the events connected with the battle of Point Pleasant, the siege of Fort Henry, Foreman's disaster, the Moravian massacre, and Crawford's campaign, together with some others which cluster closely about them, the remainder of this work will be occupied, chiefly, with brief descriptions of some of the more thrilling incidents belonging to that state of border warfare which existed for several years in the upper Ohio Valley.

Most of the descriptions will relate to acts and scenes of personal daring and bravery, which, although strictly true in point of fact, are of such marvelous character as to border almost on the wildest visions of romance.

MORGAN'S RECONTRE.

One of the earliest settlers was David Morgan, a man of great energy of character and sterling worth. He was a near relative of General Morgan, of Revolutionary memory, and like that distinguished officer, possessed in a remarkable degree, courage and capacity, for almost any emergency.

At the time we speak of, Mr. Morgan was living near Prickett's Fort, about twelve miles above Morgantown and close to the Monongahela river. He was then upward of sixty years of age, and for some days had been slightly indisposed. Early in April, 1779, he desired two of his children, Stephen, sixteen years of age, and Sarah, about fourteen, to feed the stock at his farm, distant about one mile on the opposite side of the river. This he did in consequence of feeling worse that morning than usual. No Indians had yet been seen in the neighborhood, and, of course, he considered all perfectly safe. As the weather was fine, the brother and sister concluded to remain and prepare a piece of ground for melons. Soon after they left the fort, for they were then at the stockade, Mr. Morgan lay down, and shortly falling to sleep dreamed that he saw the children walking before him scalped. This vision awoke him, and finding upon inquiry that the children had not returned, he became uneasy and started immediately in hunt of them. Approaching the premises he beheld his children busily engaged in the manner already indicated. Seating himself upon a log close at hand, Morgan watched his children for some time, when suddenly he saw emerge from the house two Indians, who moved rapidly up toward Stephen and his sister. Fearing to alarm the children, Morgan cautiously warned them of their danger and told them to go at once to the fort. They instantly obeyed, and the Indians discovering their movements, gave their accustomed whoop and started in pursuit. Morgan having hitherto escaped their attention now arose, and returning their shout caused the savages to seek behind trees instant protection.

Knowing that the chances for a fair fight were almost hopeless, Morgan thought to escape by running, and so manage as to keep the trees between himself and the enemy. In this, however, he was mistaken. Impaired health and the infirmities of age disabled him from keeping long beyond the reach of the fleet and athletic warriors. Finding after a run of some two hundred yards that the savages were rapidly gaining on him, he determined to shoot one and take his chances with the other. Turning to fire, both Indians sprang behind trees, and Morgan did the same; but finding the tree he first gained too small to protect his person, he quitted it and made for another, which was reached in safety.

One of the Indians hoping to get nearer his intended victim, ran to the tree which Morgan had left, but finding it too small, threw himself behind a log close at hand. This however did not conceal him entirely, which Morgan noticing, instantly fired, and shot the savage through the part exposed. Feeling himself mortally wounded, with more than spartan fortitude, he drew his knife and inflicted two deep stabs upon his breast. To him death had no terrors, save as dealt by the hand of his white antagonist.

The heroic old man having thus effectually disposed of one of his pursuers, again resorted to flight. The chances were now desperate, as the Indian had the double advantage of tomahawk and rifle. Running fifty or sixty yards, he glanced hurriedly over his shoulder just in time to see the savage ready to fire. Jumping to one side the ball passed harmlessly by, and the two felt that the combat must be brought to close quarters. With all the fury of his nature, the savage rushed upon his adversary with loud yells and uplifted tomahawk. Morgan prepared to meet, him with his gun, but the savage aimed a blow with his tomahawk with such force and effect, as to knock the rifle from Morgan's grasp, and cut two of the fingers from his left hand. They now clinched, and the combat became equal, except the savage was the younger and much more powerful of the two. Frantic at the loss of his companion and his own ill success, he fought with a desperation rarely known in a single combat; Morgan, on the other part, inspirited by the success which had thus far attended him, nerved his arm and strung every muscle to the conflict, resolved to kill his combatant or sell his life as dearly as possible. Our hero in his younger days had been a most, expert wrestler, and was thus enabled with ease to throw the Indian; but the latter more active and powerful, readily turned him. With a yell of exultation, the savage now held his adversary down and began to feel for his knife. Morgan saw the movement, and well knew all would be over if the savage got possession of it.

The Indian was prevented getting the knife by a woman's apron, which he had wrapped around his body in such a manner as to confine the handle. Whilst endeavoring to extricate it Morgan got one of the Indian's thumbs between his teeth, and so effectually ground it that the poor wretch was sadly disconcerted, and more than once screamed with pain. Finally he grasped his knife, but so close to the blade that Morgan, noticing it, caught the end of the handle and drew it through the Indian's hand, cutting it severely. The savage was now literally hors de combat, and springing to his feet endeavored to get away; but the resolute Morgan, not yet having done with him, held on to the thumb until he had inflicted a mortal thrust in the side of the enemy. Letting go, the Indian sank almost lifeless to the ground, and Morgan made his way to the fort. Before reaching the river he overtook his children. After hearing his adventure, a party of men left the fort and proceeded to the place of conflict. On reaching the spot nothing was to be seen of the wounded Indian; but his trail of blood indicated the place of his concealment. The poor creature had taken the knife from his side, bound up the wound with the apron already alluded to, and as the whites approached him he feelingly accosted them with "How do do, broder?" But this met with no fraternal response from the party who discovered his retreat. He was immediately dispatched, and both he and his companion were scalped.

LEWIS WETZEL'S EXPLOITS.

Lewis Wetzel was the son of John Wetzel, a German, who settled on Big Wheeling creek, about fourteen miles from the Ohio river, and was killed by the Indians near Captina, in 1777, when Lewis was about twenty three years of age. The education of Lewis, like that of his cotemporaries, was that of the hunter and warrior. When a boy he adopted the practice of loading and firing his rifle as he ran. This was the means of making him fearfully destructive to the Indians in after life. On account of his father's death, he and his brothers, of whom he had five, vowed sleepless vengeance against the whole Indian race.

During the lifetime of his father, when he was about thirteen years of age, Lewis was taken prisoner by the Indians, together with his brother Jacob, about eleven years old. Before he was taken he received a slight wound in the breast from a bullet, which carried off a small piece of his breast bone. The second night after they were taken the Indians encamped at the Big Lick, twenty miles from the river, on the waters of McMechen's creek. The boys were not confined. After the Indians had fallen asleep, Lewis whispered to his brother Jacob, that he must get up and go back home with him. Jacob at first objected, but afterwards got up and went along with him. When they had gone about one hundred yards from the camp they sat down on a log. "Well," said Lewis, "we cannot go home barefooted; I will go back and get a pair of moccasins for each of us," and accordingly did so, and returned. After sitting a little longer,

"Now," said he, "I will go back and get father's gun, and then we will start." This he effected. They had not traveled far on the trail by which they came before they heard the Indians coming after them. It was a moonlight night; when the Indians came pretty near them, they stepped aside into the bushes, let them pass then fell into the rear and traveled on. On the return of the Indians they did the same. They were then pursued by two Indians on horseback, whom they dodged in the same way. The next day they reached Wheeling in safety, crossing from the Indian shore to Wheeling Island on a raft of their own making. By this time Lewis had been almost spent from his wound.

Belmont county, Ohio, was the scene of several of the most daring adventures of this far famed borderer, two of which will be here related:

While hunting, Wetzel fell in with a young man who lived on Dunkard creek, and was persuaded to accompany him to his home. On their arrival, they found the house in ruins and all the family murdered, except a young woman who had been bred with them, and to whom the young man was ardently attached. She was taken alive, as was found by examining the trail of the enemy, who were three Indians and a white renegade. Burning with revenge, they followed the trail until opposite the mouth of Captina, where the enemy had crossed. They swam the stream and discovered the Indian camp, around the fires of which lay the enemy in careless repose. The young woman was apparently unhurt; but was making much moaning and lamentation. The young man, hardly able to restrain his rage, was for firing and rushing instantly upon them. Wetzel, more cautious, told him to wait until daylight, when there would be a better chance of success in killing the whole party. After dawn the Indians prepared to depart. The young man selecting the white renegade, and Wetzel the Indian, they both fired simultaneously with fatal effect. The young man rushed forward, knife in hand, to relieve the mistress of his affections, while Wetzel reloaded and pursued the two surviving Indians, who had taken to the woods until they could ascertain the number of their enemies. Wetzel, as soon as he was discovered, discharged his rifle at random, in order to draw them from their covert. The ruse took effect, and taking to his heels, he loaded as he ran, and suddenly wheeling about discharged his rifle through the body of his nearest and unsuspecting enemy. The remaining Indian, seeing the fate of his companion, and that his enemy's gun was unloaded, rushed forward with all energy, the prospect of prompt revenge being fairly before him. Wetzel led him on, dodging from tree to tree, until his rifle was again ready, when, suddenly turning, he fired, and his remaining enemy fell dead at his feet. After taking their scalps, Wetzel and his friend, with their rescued captive, returned in safety to the settlement.

In the year 1782, after Crawford's defeat, Lewis went with a Thomas Mills, who had been in the campaign, to get his horse, which he had left near the place where St. Clairsville now stands. At the Indian springs, two miles from St. Clairsville, on the Wheeling road, they were met by about forty Indians, who were in pursuit of the stragglers from the campaign. The Indians and white men discovered each other about the same moment Lewis fired first and killed an Indian, while the Indians wounded Mills in the heel, who was soon overtaken and killed. Four of the Indians then singled out, dropped their guns, and pursued Wetzel. Wetzel loaded his rifle as he ran. After running about half, a mile, one of the Indians, having gotten within eight or ten steps of him, Wetzel wheeled round and shot him down, ran and loaded his gun as before. After running about three quarters of a mile further, a second Indian came so close to him that when he turned to fire, the Indian caught the muzzle of his gun, and, as he expressed it, "he and the Indian had a severe wring." He, however, succeeded in bringing the muzzle to the Indian's breast and killed him on the spot. By this time, he, as well as the Indian, was pretty well tired out; yet the pursuit was continued by the two remaining Indians. Wetzel, as before, loaded his gun and stopped several times during this latter chase; when he did so the Indians treed themselves. After going something more than a mile, Wetzel took advantage of a little open piece of ground over which the Indians were passing a short distance behind him, to make a sudden stop for the purpose of shooting the foremost, who got behind a little sapling which was too small to cover his body. Wetzel shot and broke his thigh. The wound, in the issue, proved fatal. The last of the Indians then gave a little yell, and said, "No catch dat man, gun always loaded," and gave up the chase, glad no doubt to get off with his life.

It seems to be generally conceded that a most fatal decoy on the frontier was the 'turkey call.' Several anecdotes, of pretty much the same tenor, are related with reference to different parties and localities, only one of which will be here given.

On several occasions, men from the fort at Wheeling had gone across the hill in quest of a turkey whose vociferous gobbling had elicited their attention, and on more than one occasion the men never returned. Wetzel suspected the cause, and determined to satisfy himself. On the east side of the creek, at a point elevated at least sixty feet above the water, there is a small cavern the entrance to which at that time was almost obscured by a heavy growth of vines and foliage. Into this the alluring savage would crawl, and there have an extensive view of the hill front on the opposite side. From that cavern issued the decoy of death to more than one incautious soldier and settler. Wetzel knew of the existence and exact locality of the cave, and accordingly started out before day, and by a circuitous route reached the spot from the rear. Posting himself so as to command a view of the opening, he waited patiently for the expected cry. Directly the twisted tuft of an Indian warrior slowly rose in the mouth of the cave, and looking cautiously about sent forth the usual gobble, and immediately sank back out of view. Lewis screened himself in his position, cocked his gun, and anxiously awaited the reappearance of the tufted head. In a few minutes up rose the tuft, Lewis drew a fine aim on the polished head, and the next instant the brains of the savage were scattered about the cave. That turkey troubled the inhabitants no longer.

The foregoing gives only a tithe of the many hazardous exploits between the settlers and the Indians, in which Lewis Wetzel was engaged. It is said, that in the course of these wars in the upper Ohio Valley, he killed twenty seven Indians, besides a number more along the frontier settlements of Kentucky. As might naturally be supposed he was of a roving disposition. He is believed to have died at the residence of a relative named Philip Sykes, about twenty miles in the interior from Natchez.

It is said of Lewis Wetzel, that he loved his friends and hated his enemies. He belonged, like many others, to the heroic period of our country; and although rude and uncultivated in manners, it may be considered entirely within the range of probability, that his name will live in history, poetry and song to the latest posterity.

THE POE BROTHERS AND BIG FOOT.

Among those who settled at an early day in the Ohio. Valley, were two brothers, Andrew and Adam Poe. (These brothers once resided in Columbiana county, Ohio, on the West Fork of the Little Beaver. The son of Andrew, Deacon Poe, was a few wears ago living in Portage county, Ohio, near Ravenna, and owned the tomahawk with which the Indian struck his father. The locality where the struggle occurred, he informs us, was nearly opposite the mouth of Yellow Creek. Howes *Ohio Hist. Coll.)* They were born in Maryland and emigrated to the West in 1774. Andrew was the elder of the two by five years. He lived to the age of ninety three, and died in 1840.

In the summer of 1782, a party of seven Wyandottes made an incursion into a settlement some distance below Fort Pitt, and several miles from the Ohio river. Here finding an old man alone in a cabin they killed him, packed up what plunder they could find, and commenced their retreat.

Amongst their party was a celebrated Wyandotte chief, who, in addition to his fame as a warrior and counsellor, was, as to his size and strength, a real giant. This Indian was known by the name of "Big Foot."

The news of the visit of the Indians soon spread through the neighborhood, and a party of eight good riflemen was collected in a few hours for the purpose of pursuing them. In this party were the two brothers, Andrew and Adam Poe. They were both famous for courage, size and activity. This little party commenced the pursuit of the Indians with a determination, if possible, not to suffer them to escape, as they usually did on such occasions, by making a speedy flight to the river, crossing it, and then dividing into small parties to meet at a distant point in a given time. The pursuit was continued a greater part of the night after the Indians had done the mischief. In the morning, the party found themselves on the trail of the Indians which led to the river. When they arrived at a little distance from the river, Andrew Poe, fearing an ambuscade, left the party, who followed directly on the trail, to creep along the brink of the river bank under cover of the weeds and bushes, to fall on the rear of the Indians should he find them in ambuscade. He had not gone far before he saw the Indian rafts at the water's edge. Not seeing any Indians, he stepped softly down the bank with his rifle cocked. When about half way down, he discovered the large Wyandotte chief and a small Indian within a few steps of him. They were standing with their guns cocked and looking in the direction of our party, who by this time had gone some distance lower down the bottom. Poe took aim at the large chief, but his rifle missed fire. The Indians hearing the snap of the gun lock, instantly turned around and discovered Poe, who being too near them to retreat; dropped his gun and sprang from the bank upon them, and seizing the large Indian by the clothes on the breast, and, at the same time, embracing the neck of the small one, threw them both down on the ground, himself being uppermost. The small Indian soon extricated himself, ran to the raft, got his tomahawk, and attempted to dispatch Poe, the large Indian holding him fast in his arms with all his might the better to enable his fellow to effect his purpose. Poe, however, so well watched the motions of his assailant, that when in the act of aiming a blow at his head, by a vigorous and well directed kick with one of his feet, staggered the savage and knocked the tomahawk out of his hand. The failure on the part of the small Indian was reproved by an exclamation of contempt from the large one.

In a moment the Indian caught up his tomahawk again, and approached more cautiously, brandishing his tomahawk and making a number of feigned blows in defiance and derision. Poe, however, still on his guard, averted the real blow from his head by throwing up his arm and receiving it on his wrist, in which he was severely wounded, but not so as to lose entirely the use of his hand. In this perilous moment, Poe, by a violent effort broke loose from the Indian, snatched up one of the Indian's guns, and shot the small Indian through the breast as he ran up a third time to tomahawk him. The large Indian was now on his feet, and grasping Poe by the shoulder and leg threw him down on his back. Poe instantly disengaged himself and got on his feet. The Indian then seized him again, and a new struggle ensued, which, owing to the slippery state of the bank, ended in the fall of both combatants into the water. In this situation it was the object of each to drown the other. Their efforts to effect their purpose was continued for some time with alternate success, sometimes one being under the water and sometimes the other. Poe at length seized the tuft of hair on the scalp of the Indian, with which he held his head under the water until he supposed him drowned. Relaxing his hold too soon, Poe instantly found his gigantic antagonist on his feet again and ready for another combat. In this they were carried into the water beyond their depth. In this situation they were compelled to loose their hold on each other and swim for mutual safety. Both sought the shore to seize a gun and end the contest with bullets. The Indian being the best swimmer reached the land first. Poe seeing this, immediately turned back into the water to escape being shot, if possible, by diving. Fortunately the Indian caught up the rifle with which Poe killed the other warrior. At this juncture Adam Poe, missing his brother from the party, and supposing from the report of the gun which he shot, that he was either killed or engaged in conflict with the Indians, hastened to the spot. On seeing him, Andrew called out to "kill the big Indian on shore." But Adam's gun, like that of the Indian's, was empty. The contest was now between the white and the Indian, who should load and fire first. Very fortunately for Poe, the Indian in loading drew the ramrod from the thimbles of the stock of the gun with so much violence, that it slipped out of his hands and fell a little distance from him. He quickly caught it up and rammed down his bullet. This little delay gave Poe the advantage. He shot the Indian as he was raising his gun to take aim at him.

As soon as Adam had shot the Indian, he jumped into the river to assist his wounded brother to shore; but Andrew, thinking more of the scalp of the big Indian as a trophy of victory than his own safety, urged Adam to go back and prevent the struggling savage from rolling into the river and escaping. Adam's solicitude for the life of his brother prevented him from complying with this request. In the meantime, the Indian, jealous of the honor of his scalp, even in the agonies of death, succeeded in reaching the river and getting into the current, so that his body was never obtained. An unfortunate occurrence took place during the conflict. Just as Adam arrived at the top of the bank for the relief of his brother, one of the party, who had followed close behind him, seeing Andrew in the river and mistaking him for a wounded Indian, shot at him and wounded him in the shoulder. He, however, recovered from his wound. During the contest between Andrew Poe and the two Indians, the party had overtaken the remaining six of them. A desperate conflict ensued, in which five of the Indians were killed. Our loss was three men killed and Andrew Poe severely wounded. Thus ended this spartan conflict, with the loss of three valiant men on our part, and with the loss of the whole Indian party, excepting one warrior. Never on any occasion was there a greater display of desperate bravery, and seldom did a conflict take place which, in the issue, proved fatal to so great a proportion of those engaged in it.

The fatal result of this campaign, on the side of the Indians, occasioned a universal mourning among the Wyandotte nation. The big Indian and his four brothers, all of whom were killed in the same place, were among the most distinguished chiefs and warriors of their nation.

The big Indian was magnanimous as well as brave. He, more than any other individual, contributed by his example and influence to the good character of the Wyandottes for lenity towards their prisoners. He would not suffer them to be killed or ill treated. This mercy to captives was an honorable distinction in the character of the Wyandottes, and was well understood by our first settlers, who, in case of captivity, thought it a fortunate circumstance to fall into their hands.

"We have recently," says De Hass, "seen a gentleman who often witnessed Poe going through the 'fight,' and he declares the scene was the most thrilling he ever beheld. He says the old man would enter into the spirit of the conflict, and with dilated pupil, contracted muscle, and almost choked with foaming saliva, go through every motion and distinct feature of that terrible fight. He describes the appearance of these pantomimic exhibitions as most painfully interesting, and declares that the old man would be as much exhausted after the performance as though the scene had been actual."

CAPTAIN SAMUEL BRADY.

Captain Samuel Brady resided at one time in Wellsburg. He was tall, rather slender, very active, and of dark complexion. When in the forest, engaged in war or hunting, he usually wore instead of a hat, a black handkerchief bound around his head.

Towards the Indians he bore an implacable hatred, in consequence of the murder of his father and brother by them, and took a solemn oath of vengeance. To fully detail his adventures would require a volume. We have space, however, but for a few anecdotes drawn from various sources, illustrative of his courage and sagacity.

A party of Indians having made an inroad into the Sewickly settlement, committing barbarous murders and carrying off some prisoners, Brady set off in pursuit with only five men and his pet Indian. He came up with them and discovered that they were encamped on the banks of the Mahoning. Having reconnoitered their position, Brady returned to and posted his men, and in the deepest silence all awaited the break of day, when it appeared the Indians arose and stood around their fires; exulting doubtless in the scalps they had taken, the plunder they had acquired, and the injury they had inflicted on their enemies. Precarious joy, short lived triumph! The avenger of blood was beside them. At a given signal seven rifles cracked, and five Indians were dead ere they fell. Brady's well known war cry was heard, his party was among them, and the guns were all secured. The remaining Indians instantly fled and disappeared.

Brady being out with his party on one occasion, had reached Slippery Rock creek, a branch of the Beaver, without seeing signs of Indians. Here, however, he came on an Indian trail in the evening which he followed till dark without overtaking the Indians. The next morning he renewed his pursuit, and overtook them while they were engaged at their morning meal. Unfortunately for him another party of Indians were in his rear. They had fallen upon his trail and pursued him, doubtless with as much ardor as had characterized his own pursuit. At the moment he fired upon the Indians in his front, he was in turn fired upon by those in his rear. He was now between two fires and vastly outnumbered. Two of his men fell, his tomahawk was shot from his side, and the battle yell was given by the party in his rear, and loudly returned and repeated by those in his front. There was no time for hesitation, no safety in delay, no chance for successful defense in their present position. The brave captain and his rangers had to flee before their enemies, who pressed on their footsteps with no lagging speed. Brady ran towards the creek. He was known by many, if not by all of them; and many and deep were the scores to be settled between him and them. They knew the country well; he did not, and from his running towards the creek they were certain of taking him prisoner. The creek was, for a long distance above and below the point he was approaching, washed in its channel to a great depth. In the certain expectation of catching him there, the private soldiers of his party were disregarded; and throwing down their guns, and drawing their tomahawks, all pressed forward to seize their victim. Quick of eye, fearless of heart, and determined never to be a captive to the Indians, Brady comprehended their object and his only chance for escape, the moment he saw the creek; and by one mighty effort of courage and activity, defeated the one and effected the other. He sprang across the abyss of waters, and stood rifle in hand on the opposite bank in safety. As quick as lightning his rifle was primed, for it was his invariable practice, in loading, to prime first.

The next minute the powder horn was at the gun's muzzle; when, as he was in this act, a large Indian who had been foremost in the pursuit, came to the opposite bank, and with the manliness of a generous foe who scorns to undervalue the qualities of an enemy, said, in a loud voice and tolerable English, "Brady make good jump." The moment he had said so, he took to his heels and ran as crooked as a worm fence, sometimes leaping high, at others, suddenly squatting down, he appeared no way certain that Brady would not answer from the lips of his rifle. But the rifle was not yet loaded.

The Captain was at the place afterwards, and ascertained that his leap was about twenty three feet, and that the water was twenty feet deep. Brady's next effort was to gather up his men. They had a place designated at which to meet in case they should happen to be separated; and thither he went and found the other three. They immediately commenced their homeward march, and returned to Pittsburgh about half defeated. Three Indians had been seen to fall from the fire they gave them at breakfast.

Returning with John Williamson and one of the Wetzels from a successful reconnoitering expedition to Upper Sandusky, a deer track was discovered, and Brady followed it, telling the men he would perhaps get a shot at it. He had gone but a few rods when he saw the deer standing broadside to him. He raised his rifle and attempted to fire, but it flashed in the pan. He sat down, picked the touch hole, and then started on. After going a short distance the path made a bend, and he saw before him a large Indian on horseback, with a child before and its mother behind him, and a number of warriors marching in the rear. His first impulse was to shoot the Indian on horseback, but as he raised the rifle he observed the child's head roll with the motion of the horse. It was fast asleep, and tied to the Indian. He stepped behind the root of a tree, and waited until he could shoot the Indian without danger to the child or its mother.

When he considered the chance certain, he fired, and the Indian, child and mother all fell from the horse. Brady called to his men, with a voice that made the forest ring, to surround the Indians and give them a general fire. He sprang to the fallen Indian's powder horn, but could not pull it off. Being dressed like an Indian, the woman thought he was one, and said, "Why did you shoot your brother?" He caught up the child, saying, "Jenny Stoop, I am Captain Brady; follow me and I will secure you and your child." He caught her hand in his, carrying the child in the other arm, and dashed into the brush. Many guns were fired at him, but no ball touched, and the Indians dreading an ambuscade, were glad to make off. The next day he arrived at Fort McIntosh (Beavertown) with the woman and child. His men had got there before him. They had heard his war whoop, and knew they were Indians he had encountered, but having no ammunition, had taken to their heels and run off.

THE JOHNSON BROTHERS.

In the fall of 1793, two boys by the name of John and Henry Johnson, the former thirteen and the latter eleven years old, whose parents lived at Carpenter's Station, a little distance above the mouth of Short creek, on the east side of the Ohio river, were sent out in the evening to hunt the cows. At the foot of a hill, at the back of the bottom, they sat down under a hickory tree to crack some nuts. They soon saw two men coming towards them, one of whom had a bridle in his hand. Being dressed like white men, they mistook them for their father and an uncle in search of horses. When they discovered their mistake, and attempted to run off, the Indians, pointing their guns at them, told them to stop or they would kill them. They halted and were taken prisoners.

The Indians, being in pursuit of horses, conducted the boys by a circuitous route over the Short creek hills in search of them, until late in the evening, when they halted at a spring in a hollow place, about three miles from the fort. Here they kindled a small fire, cooked and ate some victuals, and prepared to repose for the night. Henry, the younger of the boys, during the ramble, had affected the greatest satisfaction at having been taken prisoner. He said his father was a hard master, who kept him always at hard work and allowed no play; but that for his part he wished to live in the woods and be a hunter. This deportment soon brought him into intimacy with one of the Indians, who could speak very good English. The Indians frequently asked the boys if they knew of any good horses running in the woods. Some time before they halted, one of the Indians gave the largest of the boys a little bag, which he supposed contained money, and made him carry it. When night came on the fire was covered up, the boys pinioned, and made to lie down together.

The Indians then placed their hoppis straps over them, and lay down, one on each side of them, on the ends of the straps. Pretty late in the night the Indians fell asleep, and one of them becoming cold, caught hold of John in his arms, and turned him over on the outside. In this situation, the boy, who had kept awake, found means to get his hands loose. He then whispered to his brother, made him get up, and untied his arms.

This done, Henry thought of nothing but running off as fast as possible; but when about to start, John caught hold of him saying: "We must kill these Indians before we go." After some hesitation, Henry agreed to make the attempt. John then took one of the rifles of the Indians and placed it on a log, with the muzzle close to the head of one of them. He then cocked the gun and placed his brother at the breech, with his finger on the trigger, and with instructions to pull it as soon as he could strike the other Indian. He then took one of the Indian's tomahawks, and standing astride of the other Indian, struck him with it. The blow, however, fell on the back of the neck and to one side, so as not to be fatal. The Indian then attempted to spring up; but the little fellow repeated his blows with such force and rapidity on the skull, that as he expressed it "the Indian lay still and began to quiver." At the moment of the first stroke given by the elder brother with the tomahawk, the younger one pulled the trigger, and shot away a considerable portion of the Indian's lower jay. The Indian, a moment after receiving the shot, began to flounce about and yell in the most frightful manner. The boys then made the best of their way to the fort, and reached it a little before daybreak. On getting near the fort they found the people all up, in great agitation on their account. On hearing a woman exclaim, "Poor little fellows, they are killed or taken prisoners!" The older one answered, "No mother we are here yet."

Having brought nothing away with them from the Indian camp, their relation of what had taken place between them and the Indians was not fully credited. A small party was soon made up to go and ascertain the truth or falsehood of their report. This party the boys conducted to the spot by the shortest route. On arriving at the place, they found the Indian whom the elder brother had tomahawked lying dead in the camp; the other had crawled away, and taken his gun and shot pouch with him. After scalping the Indian the party returned to the fort; and the same day a larger party went out to look after the wounded Indian, who had crawled some distance from the camp, and concealed himself in the top of a fallen tree, where, notwithstanding the severity of his wound, with a spartan bravery, he determined to sell his life as dearly as possible. Having fixed the gun for the purpose, on the approach of the men to a proper distance, he took aim at one of them and pulled the trigger, but his gun missed fire. On hearing the snap of the lock, one of them exclaimed, "I should not like to be killed by a dead Indian!" The party concluding that the Indian would die at any rate, thought best to retreat, and return to look for him after some time. On returning, however, he could not be found, having crawled away and concealed himself in some other place. His skeleton and gun were found sometime afterwards.

The Indians who were killed were great warriors, and very wealthy. The bag, which was supposed to contain money, it was conjectured, was found by one of the party who went out first in the morning. On hearing the report of the boys, he slipped off by himself and reached the place before the party arrived. For some time afterwards he appeared to have a great deal more money than his neighbors.

After the treaty of General Wayne, a friend of the Indians who were killed, made inquiry of a man from Short creek: "What had become of the boys who killed the Indians?" He was told that they lived at the same place with their parents. The Indian replied, "You have not done right; you should make kings of those boys."

The above account is substantially the same as that given by Henry Johnson, the younger of the two brothers, in a letter written to De Hass, in 1851. The only material point in which he differs from Doddridge is in fixing the date of the transaction in 1788, instead of 1793. The former, therefore, may be assumed as the true date. At the date of the letter referred to, Henry Johnson was a hale old man, 74 years of age, living in Monroe county, Ohio.

APPENDIX
A.

Camp Charlotte was on the right side of the Scippo, about seven miles southeast of Circleville, eight miles from old Chillicothe (now Westfall), and in sight of Pickaway Plains. Camp Lewis was on the left side of the Congo, about one and a half miles from its junction with the Scippo, and four and a half southwest of Camp Charlotte. The spot where Lord Dunmore met Gen. Lewis was on the right side of the Congo, about one mile from its junction with the Scippo, and directly opposite the residence of James Boggs, Esq. The headquarters of the Indian tribes was at Old Chillicothe, about four miles, air line, southwest of Circleville, and on the west side of the Scioto. This was Logan's home; and we have the authority of C. Whittlesey, Esq., for saying, that the interview between Col. Gibson and Logan took place "in the woods" near Old Chillicothe. But this is a disputed point. Some say it took place under a big elm tree, now standing on the farm of James Boggs, Esq., and not far from Camp Lewis. Cornstalk's town was at the lower end of the Upper Pickaway Plains, and that of the Grenadier Squaw, his sister, immediately south of that, and a little northeast of the former residence of Wm Renick, Esq. The elm tree above alluded to is now a wide spreading tree, seven feet in diameter at the base, and measuring around the tips of its largest branches three hundred and seventy feet. This tree was recognized in later years by some of the soldiers of Lord

Dunmore, and by it they were enabled to identify almost the exact spot of meeting between his Lordship and General Lewis.

B.

Simon Girty was a renegade white man, who, for some cause, had taken offense against his own people, and for the purpose of revenge, had allied himself to the British cause. He was present at the treaty of Lord Dunmore with the Indians; and, it is said, maintained at that time and subsequently very intimate and confidential relations with his Lordship. He was also present at the burning of Crawford; commanded at the battle of Bluelicks, Ky., in the year 1778; was at St. Clair's defeat; also, at Proctor's defeat; and according to one account, was then cut to pieces by Col. Johnson's mounted men. But another account is, that he became blind four years before his death. He had three brothers with the Indians, James, Joseph, and George. These facts are derived from Howe's *Ohio Historical Collections*.

C.

A very different version of the powder exploit from that given by Mr. McKiernan and others, is contained in the following letter from Mrs. Lydia S. Cruger:

[From DeHass' *History of the Indian Wars*.]

"The undersigned having been applied to for a statement of facts respecting the memorable achievement at the attack on Fort Henry (Wheeling), in September, 1782, known as the gunpowder exploit, would state as follows, viz:

"On Monday afternoon, September 11, 1782, a body of about 300 Indians and 50 British soldiers, composing part of a Company known as the Queen's Rangers, appeared in front of the fort and demanded a surrender. These forces were commanded respectively by the white renegade Girty and Captain Pratt. The demand for a surrender was of course not complied with, and the attack then commenced.

"During the forenoon of Tuesday, September 12th, the enemy having temporarily withdrawn from the attack, but occupying a position within gunshot of the fort, those within the stockade observed a female leave the residence of Colonel Zane and advance with rapid movements toward the fort. She made for the southern gate, as it was less exposed to the fire of the enemy. The gate was opened immediately and she entered in safety. That person was none other than Mollie Scott, and the object of her mission was to procure powder for those who defended the dwelling of Colonel Zane. The undersigned was, at that time, in her seventeenth year, and remembers every circumstance connected with the incident. She saw Mollie Scott enter the fort, assisted her in getting the powder, and saw her leave; and avers most positively that she, and she alone, accomplished the feat referred to, and deserves all the credit that may be attached to it.

"The ammuuition at that time was kept in the store house adjoining the residence of my father, and known as the 'Captain's house.' My father (Captain Boggs) having left for help on the commencement of the attack, and I being the oldest child under the parental roof, was directed by my mother to go with the messenger (Mollie Scott) to the store house, and give her whatever ammunition she needed. This the undersigned did, and will now state without fear of contradiction, that the powder was given to Mollie Scott, and not to Elizabeth Zane. The undersigned assisted Mollie Scott in placing the powder in her apron, and to this she is willing to be qualified at any time.

"Elizabeth Zane, for whom has long been claimed the credit of this heroic feat, was at the residence of her father, near the present town of Washington, Pa. At the time of its occurrence, the achievement was not considered very extraordinary. Those were emphatically times when woman's heart was nerved to deeds of no ordinary kind. We all felt it was then 'to do or die,' and the undersigned does not hesitate to say, that more than one within the little stockade at Wheeling would have accomplished the feat with as much credit as the one whose name seems destined to an immortality in border warfare.

"But the undersigned does not wish to detract from the heroism of the act; she only desires to correct a gross error, to give honor to whom honor is due. This she deems imperative, that the truth and justice of history may be maintained.

"The undersigned disclaims all unkind feeling toward any one in relation to this statement. Elizabeth Zane was one of her earliest acquaintances, whom she knew to be a woman brave, generous and single hearted.

"Given under my hand and seal, this 28th day of November, 1849.

"LYDIA S. CRUGER, [Seal.]"

Mrs. Cruger seems to have attached but very little importance to the matter in question, until she saw in print what she always indignantly denounced as a perverted statement of the facts. The writer has more than once heard her do this, in no measured terms. She felt called upon, as she says, from a sense of duty, to maintain the facts of history, and came out in print over her own signature, giving what she claimed to be a true version of the affair.

If the statement of Mrs. Cruger is to be considered reliable, then, so far at least as Elizabeth Zane is concerned, the story as given by Mr. McKeirnan and others may be regarded as a very pretty bit of romance, resting on no sufficient evidence.

That the main facts as given by the writers referred to in regard to the powder exploit are true, there can be no reasonable doubt. But that Mollie Scott, and not Elizabeth Zane, was the real heroine in the case, is positively affirmed by Mrs. Cruger. Nor will it be a very easy matter to set her testimony aside.

Mrs. Cruger was the daughter of Captain William Boggs, who, at the time of the siege, had charge of the public stores within the stockade, but was temporarily absent hunting up supplies. She was then seventeen years of age, and retained to the day of her death a vivid impression of the events she records. Her first husband was Colonel Moses Shepherd, son of the commandant. She subsequently married Colonel Cruger, of New York, at one time member of Congress, and died a few years ago at the Monument House, six miles east of Wheeling, on the National road, at the age of 102 years. She was a lady of remarkably sound judgment and retentive memory, and it is yet to be learned that her character for veracity has ever been successfully impeached. Mrs. Colonel Fremont, saw Mrs. Cruger when she was 100 years old, and speaks of her mind as being at that time, perfectly clear and vigorous. Her account of the transaction referred to, has the merit of being clear, circumstantial, positive and almost defiant. It is not given as hearsay evidence merely, but as a narrative of events which fell under her own personal observation, and in which she was to some extent an active participant.

Withers, the *Ohio Historical Collections*, and other authorities, concur with Mrs. Cruger in fixing the date of the powder transaction in the year 1782, and there is good reason to believe that this is correct. McKeirnan, who perhaps started the error, that the siege of Fort Henry was in 1777, admits in a letter to the writer, that 1782 was probably the true date. As to the numerous statements and theories which have been put afloat of late years in prose, poetry and fiction, with the view of invalidating the testimony of Mrs. Cruger, the writer would say, with due respect to their authors, that there are obvious reasons why they should be received with a considerable degree of allowance. With these remarks he submits the matter to the judgment of a candid public.

D.

It should be stated, that in the year 1781, the British had, under an escort of three hundred warriors, caused the Moravians to be removed to Detroit, on the pretext of giving them greater security and protection, but really to discover if they were favorable to the American cause.

Finding no reason to suspect them, one hundred and fifty of them were allowed to return to their towns and gather their corn. The remainder were located at Upper Sandusky under guard of the Delawares, to be plundered, and to eke out a miserable existence during the winter. It was of the one hundred and fifty that returned to their towns, that ninety six were murdered, the rest making their escape. After the massacre, in 1782, they were all removed to the Scioto.